History Makers

Florence Nightingale

... and a new age of nursing

Sarah Ridley

W

FRANKLIN WATTS
LONDON·SYDNEY

First published in 2009 by
Franklin Watts
338 Euston Road
London NW1 3BH

Franklin Watts Australia
Level 17/207 Kent Street
Sydney NSW 2000

Series editor: Jeremy Smith
Art director: Jonathan Hair
Design: Simon Morse
Cover design: Jonathan Hair
Picture research: Sarah Ridley

Picture credits: Bettmann/Corbis: front
cover left. The Bridgeman Art Library/
Getty Images: 13. C P Cushing/
Classicstock/Topfoto: front cover right.
Florence Nightingale Museum, London,
UK/Bridgeman Art Library: 20.
Hulton Archive/Getty Images: 15.
© NPG London: 9. Picturepoint/ Topham:
8, 14, 16, 21. The Print Collector/
HIP/Topfoto: 22. H Armstrong
Roberts/Classicstock/Topfoto: 1.
Stone/Getty Images: 4. Topfoto: 23.
Wellcome Picture Library: 5, 6, 7, 10, 11, 12,
18, 19. World History Archive/Topfoto: 17.

Dewey classification: tbc
ISBN 978 0 7496 8707 6

A CIP catalogue record for this book is
available from the British Library

Printed in China

Franklin Watts is a division of
Hachette Children's Books, an
Hachette Livre UK company.
www.hachettelivre.co.uk

Contents

The family

In 1818, William and Frances Nightingale decided to go travelling in Europe. While they were in Italy they had two daughters.

 Many wealthy people took long holidays at this time, visiting Florence in Italy (above) and other places.

1818 ▶

September
1819 ▶

William and Frances Nightingale marry.

Parthenope is born.

This painting shows Florence (right), Parthenope and their mother.

The first daughter was born in Naples in 1819. She was named after the old name for the city, Parthenope. Florence was born in 1820 when her parents were living in Florence.

May
1819

January
1820

12 May
1820

Victoria (later to be **Queen Victoria**) is born.

George III dies. George IV becomes king.

Florence is born.

Early life

Soon the family returned to England. They shared their time between two homes; Lea Hurst and later, Embley Park.

▲ Lea Hurst in Derbyshire - one of the Nightingales' homes.

1821 ▶

The Nightingale family returns to England.

Many cousins and friends visited the Nightingales at Embley Park.

Florence and Parthenope grew up in comfort. They were educated by a governess, and later by their father. He was wealthy so he did not need to work.

June
1825 ▶

The Nightingales buy Embley Park in Hampshire.

October
1825 ▶

The first steam-powered public railway opens.

7

Growing up

 Florence (sitting) and Parthenope, like all young ladies, learnt how to sew.

Florence was clever and soon impressed people with what she knew. Her mother loved holding parties. She hoped her daughters would meet rich young men and marry them.

1829

The first police force is set up in London.

1830

George IV dies. William IV becomes king.

Florence found the parties dull. She wanted to do something with her life rather than become someone's wife.

A drawing of Richard Monckton Milnes, who asked Florence to marry him several times. She refused him (see page 11).

1833 ▶

Working hours in factories are reduced.

1837 ▶

Queen Victoria becomes queen.

9

A calling from God

One day Florence was in the garden at Embley Park when she had a strange feeling. She felt that God was telling her to do His work, and to care for sick people and make them better.

 Florence saved this tiny owl from boys who were hurting it.

1837 ▶

Florence's religious experience at the age of 17.

1837-1839 ▶

Florence travels around Europe with her family.

This Victorian cartoon shows a nurse. Most nurses were old women with little training.

Her parents were against the idea but Florence was determined. She spent as much time as she could visiting sick people and reading about nursing.

1840 ▶

Queen Victoria marries Prince Albert.

1842 ▶

Florence meets Richard Monckton Milnes.

1849 ▶

Florence says she cannot marry Monckton Milnes.

Nursing at last

In 1851 Florence's father finally let her train to be a nurse at a German hospital. Then he hoped that she would come home, get married and settle down.

 Florence spent three months at the Kaiserswerth training hospital (above) in western Germany learning about nursing.

1851 ▶

Florence spends three months training to be a nurse.

August
1853 ▶

Florence gets a job at a London hospital.

Instead Florence got a nursing job at a hospital for sick women in London. She spent her time there, or in orphanages or schools.

These children went to a **ragged school** for poor children. Florence taught in a ragged school.

October
1853 ▶

The Crimean War begins between Russia and Turkey.

The Crimean War

Many died or were wounded at the Battle of the Alma, in the Crimea, in 1854.

In 1854 Britain and France joined Turkey in a war against Russia in the **Crimea**. Florence heard about the suffering of the British soldiers and wanted to help.

March
1854

Britain joins the Crimean War.

May
1854

Florence's 34th birthday.

14

Luckily, one of her friends, Sidney Herbert, was a **politician**. He asked her to take a group of nurses out to Turkey to see what she could do for the soldiers.

Sidney Herbert thought Florence would be able to improve the army's hospital.

September
1854 ▶

Battle of the Alma in the Crimea.

October
1854 ▶

Newspapers report the terrible state of British army hospitals in Turkey.

To Scutari

Florence and 38 nurses travelled to the army hospital at Scutari in Turkey. Soon, hundreds of wounded soldiers arrived at the hospital.

The army hospital at Scutari. Florence found few doctors and filthy wards there.

November
1854 ▶
Florence and the nurses arrive at Scutari.

March
1855 ▶
British officials organise for the **sewers** under Scutari hospital to be cleaned out.

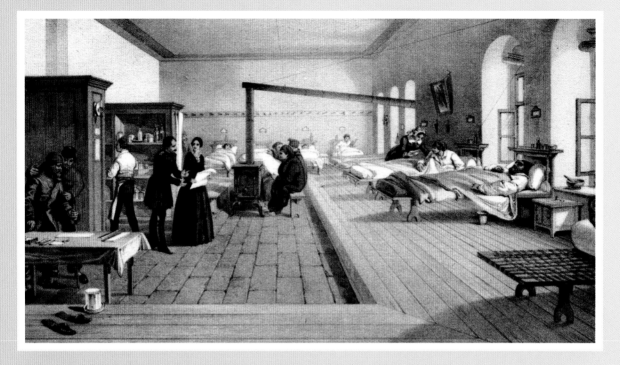

Florence made sure the sheets were washed and the wards cleaned.

Florence and the nurses set to work. They cleaned the filthy hospital, organised supplies of medicines and cared for the soldiers.

April
1855 ▶
More soldiers start to recover.

1855 ▶
Florence is very ill but recovers.

The lady with the lamp

Florence and her nurses improved the care of the soldiers, wrote letters home for them and treated them kindly.

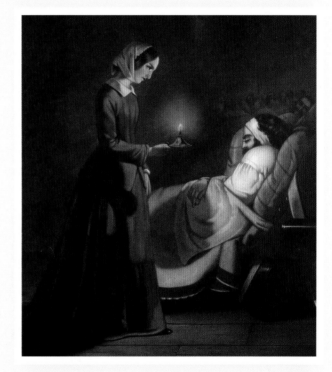

The soldiers called Florence 'the lady with the lamp', as she carried a lantern through the wards at night.

March
1856

The Crimean War ends. Russia loses.

18

When the war ended in 1856, the nurses returned home. Florence was famous back in Britain but she was angry that she had not been able to save more soldiers' lives.

This drawing of Florence was illustrated after she returned from the Crimean War.

August
1856

Florence returns to England with her nurses.

September
1856

Florence goes back to her family home.

19

Hospitals

Florence went to live in London. She was often ill but always busy. She wrote letters and talked to powerful people about improving army hospitals around the world.

The Nightingale Training School for Nurses was set up at St Thomas' Hospital in 1860.

1858

Parthenhope marries
Sir Harry Verney.

1860

Nightingale Training
School opens.

Florence sits surrounded by Nightingale nurses in 1886.

Soon Florence was working out how to improve British hospitals. She helped set up a school of nursing at St Thomas' Hospital in London.

September
1860 ▷
Florence's book *Notes on Nursing* is published.

December
1861 ▷
Prince Albert, Queen Victoria's husband, dies.

Old age

When she was almost 70, Florence started to go out and see more people. She continued to write books, letters and reports in her London flat and visited Parthenhope at her large home.

Florence wrote hundreds of letters, many of which have survived.

1874 ▶
Florence's father dies.

1880 ▶
Florence's mother dies.

1890 ▶
Florence's sister, Parthenhope, dies.

Florence lived to the age of 90.
We remember her for her work
in the Crimea and for improving
nursing around the world.

Friends and family cared for Florence when she was old.

Glossary

Crimean War (1853-1856)
The war between Britain, France and Turkey on one side, Russia on the other.

Governess A woman who taught rich children in their own home.

Politician Someone whose job it is to help run the government.

Prince Albert (1819-1861) Queen Victoria's husband.

Queen Victoria (1837-1901) Queen of Britain during Florence's lifetime.

Ragged schools Free schools for poor children. Most children didn't go to school as their parents couldn't afford to pay.

Sewers Drainage pipes and tunnels to carry away dirty water and waste.

Ward The name for a room full of beds and patients in a hospital.

Index